BLESSED NAMES

WHY WAS SHE NAMED FATIMAH (A)?

WRITTEN BY:
KISA KIDS PUBLICATIONS

Please recite a Fātiḥah for the marḥūmīn
of the Rangwala family, the sponsors of this book.

All proceeds from the sale of this book
will be used to produce more educational resources.

Dedication

This book is dedicated to the beloved Imām of our time (AJ). May Allāh (swt) hasten his reappearance and help us become his true companions.

Acknowledgements

Prophet Muḥammad (s): The pen of a writer is mightier than the blood of a martyr.

True reward lies with Allāh, but we would like to sincerely thank Shaykh Salim Yusufali and Sisters Sabika Mitha Liliana Villalvazo, Zahra Sabur, Kisae Nazar, Sarah Assaf, Nadia Dossani, Fatima Hussain, Naseem Rangwala, a Zehra Abbas. We would especially like to thank Nainava Publications for their contributions. May Allāh bless them this world and the next.

Preface

Prophet Muḥammad (s): Nurture and raise your children in the best way. Raise them with the love of the Proph and the Ahl al-Bayt (a).

Literature is an influential form of media that often shapes the thoughts and views of an entire generation. Therefc in order to establish an Islamic foundation for the future generations, there is a dire need for compelling Isla literature. Over the past several years, this need has become increasingly prevalent throughout Islamic centers a schools everywhere. Due to the growing dissonance between parents, children, society, and the teachings of Isl and the Ahl al-Bayt (a), this need has become even more pressing. Al-Kisa Foundation, along with its subsidia Kisa Kids Publications, was conceived in an effort to help bridge this gap with the guidance of ʿulamah and the hel educators. We would like to make this a communal effort and platform. Therefore, we sincerely welcome construc feedback and help in any capacity.

The goal of the *Blessed Names* series is to help children form a lasting bond with the 14 Māʿṣūmīn by learr about and connecting with their names. We hope that you and your children enjoy these books and use them a means to achieve this goal, inshā'Allāh. We pray to Allāh to give us the strength and tawfīq to perform our duties responsibilities.

With Duʾās,
Nabi R. Mir (Abidi)

Kisa Kids Publications
4415 Fortran Court
San Jose, CA 95134
(260) KISA-KID [547-2543]

An Introduction to the Blessed Names

Our names are a very special part of us. Many times, they shape our personalities and even explain who we are or the person we would like to become. In this series, you will explore the names and titles of our beloved 14 Ma'soomeen. Did you know that their names and titles were not just ordinary names? They were special because they were given to them by Allah!

Allah has given seven special heavenly names to our Ma'soomeen: Muhammad, Ali, Fatimah, Hasan, Husain, Ja'far, and Musa. Behind each of these names is a heavenly power!

In addition to their names, each of the Ma'soomeen also had special titles by which they became famous. Their titles were often given to them because of the circumstances of their time, but these titles and characteristics were common amongst all the Ma'soomeen. For example, Imam al-Baqir (a) was known for spreading knowledge because he was able to create many new universities and branches of knowledge during his time. However, if the other Ma'soomeen had the same opportunity, they, too, would have spread knowledge and created universities in their teaching circles. In these stories, you will discover some of the reasons why the Ma'soomeen received their specific names or titles.

Many of us share our names with these beloved Ma'soomeen or know people who do. Let's learn about these blessed names and titles so we can strive to be like our blessed Ma'soomeen!

I think Fatimah means....

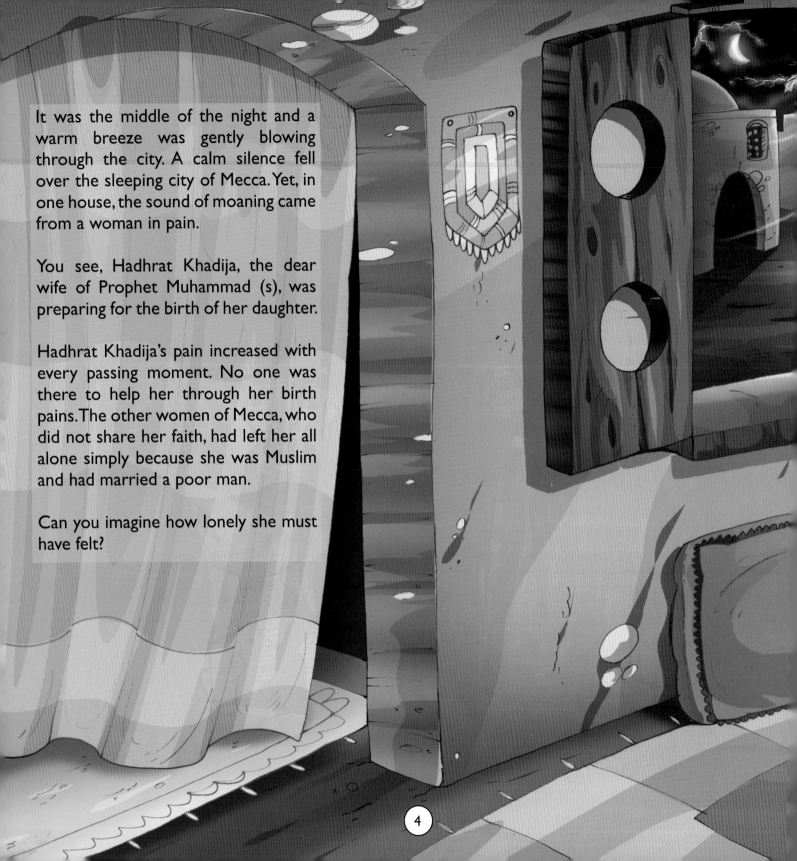

It was the middle of the night and a warm breeze was gently blowing through the city. A calm silence fell over the sleeping city of Mecca. Yet, in one house, the sound of moaning came from a woman in pain.

You see, Hadhrat Khadija, the dear wife of Prophet Muhammad (s), was preparing for the birth of her daughter.

Hadhrat Khadija's pain increased with every passing moment. No one was there to help her through her birth pains. The other women of Mecca, who did not share her faith, had left her all alone simply because she was Muslim and had married a poor man.

Can you imagine how lonely she must have felt?

All of a sudden, the skies of Mecca split open, and Hadhrat Khadija found herself surrounded by four women. Allah had sent these very special, heavenly women to help and comfort Hadhrat Khadija. By her side were Sarah, the wife of Prophet Ibrahim (a); Asiyah, the pious wife of the evil Pharaoh; Mariam, the mother of Prophet Isa (a); and Kulthum, the sister of Prophet Musa (a).

Soon, Hadhrat Khadija gave birth to a beautiful baby girl named Fatimah, a name that Allah had chosen for her.

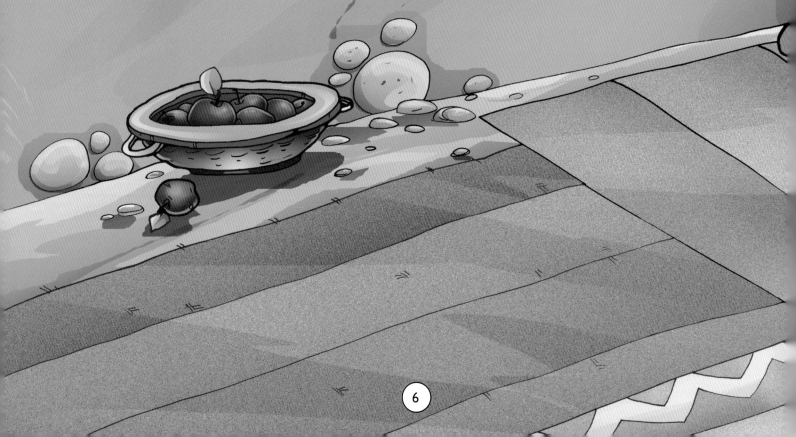

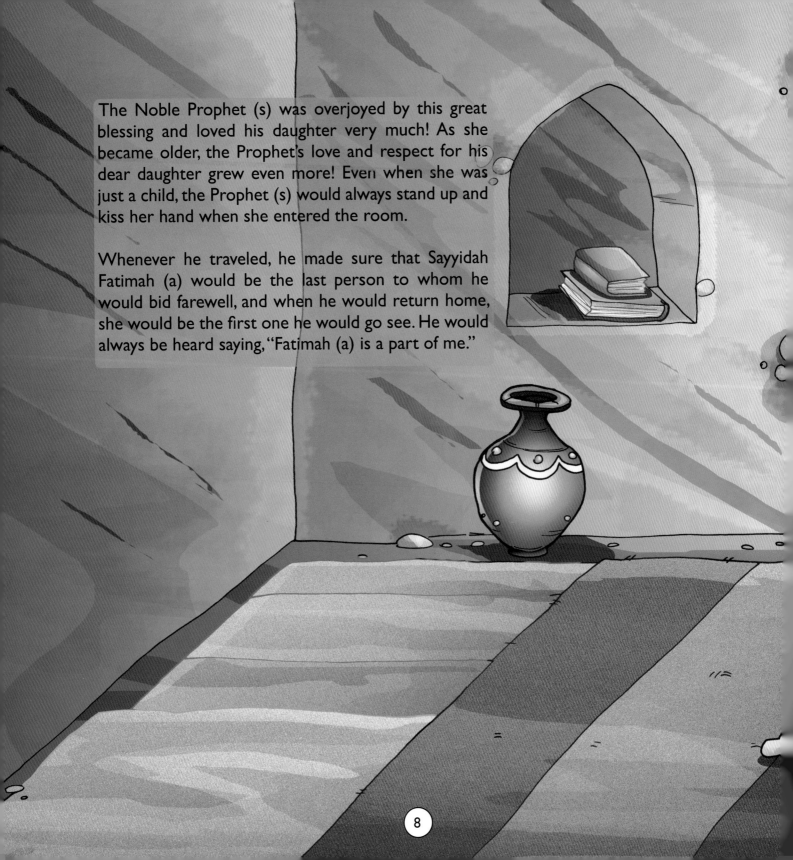

The Noble Prophet (s) was overjoyed by this great blessing and loved his daughter very much! As she became older, the Prophet's love and respect for his dear daughter grew even more! Even when she was just a child, the Prophet (s) would always stand up and kiss her hand when she entered the room.

Whenever he traveled, he made sure that Sayyidah Fatimah (a) would be the last person to whom he would bid farewell, and when he would return home, she would be the first one he would go see. He would always be heard saying, "Fatimah (a) is a part of me."

Years later, Hadhrat Khadija became ill and passed away. The Prophet (s) was very sad; now, he only had Sayyidah Fatimah (a). During those difficult days, Sayyidah Fatimah (a) would show even more love and affection towards her father.

When the disbelievers would hurt her father, she would help bandage his wounds. The Prophet's love for his daughter continued to increase with each passing day.

People soon began to wonder why the Prophet (s) loved and respected his daughter so much. They would ask each other, "What makes her so special?"

One day, Allah told Prophet Muhammad (s) to tell the people of Mecca that they should call him "Rasulullah," meaning the messenger of Allah, instead of "Muhammad." Everyone, even Sayyidah Fatimah (a) obeyed this command.

However, one day, when Sayyidah Fatimah (a) said to her father, "O Rasulullah," he replied to her, "O my daughter, this order of Allah does not include you. You are from me, and I am from you. Please call me 'dear father.' These words make Allah happier and bring joy to my heart."

Years passed and Sayyidah Fatimah (a) became a young lady. It was now time for her to get married. The rich leaders from Medina came to ask for her hand in marriage, but none of them were good enough to marry her. Sayyidah Fatimah (a) married the only person who was worthy of her: Imam Ali (a).

Sayyidah Fatimah (a) and Imam Ali (a) lived in a peaceful and loving home. Allah blessed them with four beautiful children. Even though taking care of her children and doing all the household chores was difficult, Sayyidah Fatimah (a) never complained.